5 STEP ENGLISH
Snow White

5단계로 술술 읽히는 영어원서
단계 영어 백설공주

초　　판 | 1쇄 발행 2025년 10월 20일

원 작 자 | 빌헬름 그림, 야코프 그림
영어번역 | Steve Oh
그　　림 | 이은진
정보맵핑 | 이야기 연구소
디 자 인 | 아름다운디자인
감　　수 | HannahAllyse Kim / Edmund Nai
제 작 처 | 다온피앤피
특허등록 | 10-2717987
국제출원 | PCT/KE202/002551

펴 낸 곳 | (주)도서출판동행
펴 낸 이 | 오승근
출판등록 | 2020년 3월 20일 제2020-000005호
주　　소 | 부산광역시 부산진구 동천로 109, 9층
이 메 일 | withyou@withyoubooks.com
카카오톡 | @동행출판사

단계별 요약정보 기술은 국내특허등록 및 PCT 국제출원을 했습니다.

이 책은 저작권법에 따라 보호받는 저작물이므로 무단 전재와 복제를 금지하며,
이 책 내용의 전부 또는 일부를 이용하려면 반드시 출판사의 서면 동의를 받아야 합니다.
잘못된 책은 구입하신 서점에서 바꿔 드립니다.

ISBN 979-11-91648-48-5(13740)

5단계로 **술술 읽히는** 영어원서

단계영어

백설공주

머리말
Prologue

언어 실력이 자라날수록,
영어책도 함께 자라야 합니다.

아이에게 신발이나 옷을 사줄 때 한 치수 크게 고르는 이유가 뭘까요? 바로 아이가 빠르게 자라기 때문입니다. 사실 아이의 신체만큼이나 머릿속 사고력도 금방 자라납니다. 그리고 사고력이 자랄수록, 아이가 접하는 영어책도 함께 '성장'해야 합니다.

어린 나뭇가지를 그냥 두면 제멋대로 휘어 자라지만, 어릴 때 곧은 부목으로 지지해주면 올곧게 자라는 것처럼, 아이의 학습도 비슷합니다. 매번 나무를 뽑고 더 큰 나무를 새로 심기보다는, 하나의 나무를 끝까지 가꾸는 법을 알려주는 편이 훨씬 좋습니다. 이 책도 같은 맥락에서 시작되었습니다. **하나의 스토리를 아이 수준에 맞춰 5단계로 발전시키는 신개념 영어 도서이니까요.**

아이들이 말을 배워가는 과정을 떠올려보세요. 처음에는 "엄마", "아빠"처럼 단 몇 단어만 말하지만, 시간이 흐를수록 말이 길어지고 내용도 깊어집니다. 예를 들어, 처음엔 "엄마 밥 줘"라고 말하던 아이가 나중에는 "엄마, 내가 좋아하는 김밥 먹고 싶어요"라고 표현하게 되죠. 중요한 것은 표현이 달라져도 "배가 고파서 음식을 먹고 싶다"는 핵심은 같다는 사실입니다.

이 책의 5단계 영어 구성은 바로 이런 언어 발달 과정을 그대로 담았습니다. 예를 들어, 레벨1은 네 살 아이의 표현, 레벨2는 다섯 살 아이의 표현과 비슷하다고 볼 수 있습니다. **전하고자 하는 메시지는 같지만, 표현 방식은 점점 더 풍부해지는 것이죠.**

계단을 오르듯이 레벨별로 차근차근 읽어보세요. 아이의 사고력과 함께 영어 실력도 자연스럽게 자라날 것입니다.

Steve Oh

머리말
Prologue

When you buy shoes or clothes for your child, you often choose a size up because you know they're going to grow. Children's thoughts expand just as quickly, so it makes sense for their English books to evolve as well.

If young twigs aren't supported, they'll grow bent and crooked. However, if you straighten a branch that has fallen to the ground by tying it to a sturdy splint, it will grow upright. Children are no different. Instead of uprooting a sapling to plant a bigger one, teach them to care for the tree they have. This book presents a new approach: it unfolds a story in five stages tailored to different reading levels.

Think about how children learn to speak. A child who can only say "mom" or "dad" soon starts to form longer words and more meaningful sentences. They might first say, "Give me food, Mom," but later, that evolves into something like "Mom, I want to eat my favorite food, gimbap." Even though the words change, the intention—"I'm hungry" or "I want to eat"—remains the same.

In 5 Step English, the natural course of a child's language development—what usually takes three to four years—has been divided into five levels. Level 1 reflects the way a typical four-year-old might speak; Level 2 matches a five-year-old, and so on. The core idea stays consistent, but the complexity of the expression increases with each level.

I encourage you to read through each level as though you're climbing a set of steps, one at a time.

Steve Oh

독자후기
Reviews

크라우드펀딩을 통해 책을 받은 독자들의 실제 후기입니다.

"학생을 가르치는 선생님으로 이런 책들이 많이 나왔으면 좋겠어요. 단계별로 챕터를 넘어가면서 조금씩 읽는 부분들이 늘어나는 게 보여서 뿌듯합니다!"

- 신천동 안수진

"아이에게 공부해라 잔소리하지 않고 엄마도 같이 읽을 수 있어서 효율적이네요. , 아이가 "이게 이런 이야기였어?" 하네요. 다른 동화도 출판되면 좋겠습니다."

- 춘천시 은고래

"조카들이랑 읽는 중입니다. 같은 내용이라도 단계별로 글 밥이 조금씩 늘어나서 읽는 즐거움이 있어요. 시중에 있는 동화책들은 조카들이 읽는 단계에선 내용이 너무 단순해 재미없어했는데, **단계별 영어 동화는 단계별로 문장이 늘어나서 읽는 재미가 있다고 하네요.** 또 다른 동화책 언제 나오나요? 기다리고 있습니다!"

- 제주도 봄나무

"너무 좋아요! 영어 공부에 원서 읽기가 도움이 된다고 해서 샀는데 단계별로 업그레이드해서 읽을 수 있으니까 너무 좋습니다. ."

- 반곡동 로즈

"책에 삽화들도 너무 예뻐서 소장 가치도 높고, 단계별로 글자 크기도 다른 것을 보면서 정말 섬세하다고 느꼈습니다. 영어원서 도전하실 분들!! 이 책을 적극 추천합니다!!"

- 연지동 NAZ

"저는 결혼한 지 4년 차 되는 사람입니다. 평소에 영어에 대한 관심이 많아 다양한 방법으로 영어 공부를 했습니다. 그러다가 단계 영어를 알게 되었습니다. 자세히 읽어보고 마음에 들어 다른 단계 영어 도서도 구매했습니다. 단계 영어는 아주 만족스럽습니다. 앞으로 자녀와 함께 읽을 생각으로 동행에서 출간하는 단계 영어를 계속 구매할 예정입니다. 물론 아내도 아주 만족하고 함께 읽고 이야기하고 있습니다.

- 달안동 **조청휘**

단계 영어는 총 5레벨로 구성되어 있어요. 레벨 1을 펼치는 순간 너무 만만해 보여서 신이 나더군요. 그래서 단숨에 읽어버렸습니다. 2단계부터는 문장이 추가되어 내용이 풍부해집니다. 2단계도 중학교 1학년 영어 단어를 알고 있다면 수월하게 넘어갑니다. 초등학교 3학년 아들에게 **잠자리 동화로 레벨 1을 읽어 주었어요.** 「백설공주」 내용을 알고 있는 터라 큰 거부감 없이 듣더군요. 중간중간 단어 질문을 했지만 지겨워하진 않았어요. 5단계는 다 읽는 데 시간이 걸렸지만, 사전을 찾지는 않았어요. 사전을 찾는 게 귀찮기도 했지만, 대충의 내용을 알고 있으니 모르는 단어는 느낌으로 넘겼어요. **공부가 아니라 그야말로 책 읽기를 한 것이죠.** 영어책 한 권을 이렇게 다 읽어본 게 언제인지 모르겠네요. 자신감이 붙어서 아주 좋았어요. 특히나 1단계는 아이와 함께 읽을 수 있어 더 좋았습니다.

- 창원시 **줄라이안**

"책이 1단계부터 5단계까지로 구성되어 있어 제 수준에 맞춰 읽을 수 있다는 점이 아주 만족스럽습니다. 첫 책인 「어린 왕자」부터 「노인과 바다」, 「백설공주」까지 삽입된 그림도 아기자기해서 소장용으로도 좋습니다."

-중구 **책읽는 사람**

"1단계를 읽을 때는 너무 쉬워서 마음 편히 읽었는데, 2단계부터는 저도 모르게 영어사전을 찾더라고요. 하지만 사전을 보지 않고 문단 앞뒤를 유추해서 읽었는데, 무리 없이 이해되었어요. 저처럼 '영알못'인 성인들께 추천합니다."

- 탕정면 **임나경**

독자후기
Reviews

"여섯 살 쌍둥이 엄마예요. 아이들을 키우면서 몸과 마음이 지치고 책 한 권도 못 보는 시간이 너무 길었어요. 와디즈에서 보고 저도 공부 좀 하고 아이들에게도 읽어주면 좋겠다는 생각에 펀딩했어요. 아직 1, 2레벨 정도 읽고 있지만, 흥미를 느끼게 하고 점점 욕심나게 하는 책이네요. 발음이 좋지는 않지만, 아이들도 그림을 보면서 재미있어합니다. 다양한 책을 읽게 해도 좋겠지만, 한 책을 반복해서 계속 읽어주는 것도 좋을 것 같아요. 이 책은 아이들이 초등학교에 가서도 보여주려고 합니다. 물론 그전에 제가 먼저 완독해야겠죠?"

- 문래동 **천진맘**

"1단계를 읽어 보시면 너무 쉬워서 당황스러우실 거예요. 제가 영작하는 수준(?)이지만 당장 영작해 줄 수는 없는! (영어의 신비... oTL) 아이들에게 핵심만 전달하는 영어 문장! 아이가 다섯 살이어도 접근할 수 있으니, '엄마표 영어'에 뜻이 있는 어머님들은 부담 없이 도전해 보세요. 유아용 영어 책 말고는 이 책이 첫 '이야기'인데요, 노래를 넘어 읽기도 좋아하는 아이가 되길 바라며 선택했습니다. 저도 아직 1단계밖에 못 읽었지만, 아이와 함께 자랄 문장이 기대돼요. :)"

- 제주도 **봄나무**

사용설명서
Manual

단계 영어
오디오 채널

영어는 언어입니다. 그래서 단순 암기보단, **실제 사용을 통해 익혀야 합니다.** 즉, 의미가 있어야 하고 내가 사용해야 합니다. 이 책은 학습지가 아닌, 책으로써 영어를 의미 있게 사용할 수 있게 제작했습니다.

간단하지만 명확하게 도서 사용 방법을 말씀드리겠습니다.

1. 영어 공부가 아닌 **책을 읽는다고 생각**하세요.

2. **레벨 1부터 읽으세요.** 레벨 1이 무척 쉽게 보여도 일단 레벨 1부터 읽어야 다음 단계로 수월하게 올라갈 수 있습니다. 마치 계단을 오를 때, 첫 계단에 발을 내디디고 그다음 계단으로 오르는 것처럼 말입니다.

3. 모르는 단어가 보여도 사전[1]을 찾지 마세요. 다시 한 번 말씀드리지만, 이 건 입니다. 책은 읽어야 합니다. 우리가 보통 책을 읽을 때 국어사전을 찾으면서 읽지 않는 것처럼 말입니다.

4. 레벨 5까지 읽었다면 이제 레벨 4, 3 순으로 거꾸로 읽어 보세요. 복잡한 문들이 어떻게 간략하게 요약되는지를 배울 수 있게 됩니다.

자, 그럼 이제 시작해 볼까요?

---

[1] 레벨5 에서는 사전을 찾으셔도 됩니다. 이 때는 내용 이해를 위해서가 아닌 모르는 단어의 정확한 의미 파악을 위해 사전을 찾을 필요가 있습니다.

목 차
Contents

단계 영어
오디오북 채널

머리말

독자 후기

도서 사용법

Snow White **LEVEL 1** — 10

Chapter 1	12
Chapter 2	14
Chapter 3	22
Chapter 4	28
Chapter 5	36
Chapter 6	43

Snow White **LEVEL 2** — 48

Chapter 1	50
Chapter 2	52
Chapter 3	60
Chapter 4	68
Chapter 5	77
Chapter 6	82

Snow White **LEVEL 3**	**88**
Chapter 1	90
Chapter 2	92
Chapter 3	98
Chapter 4	105
Chapter 5	111
Chapter 6	116

Snow White **LEVEL 4**	**120**
Chapter 1	122
Chapter 2	124
Chapter 3	128
Chapter 4	132
Chapter 5	140
Chapter 6	145

Snow White **LEVEL 5**	**148**
Chapter 1	150
Chapter 2	152
Chapter 3	160
Chapter 4	165
Chapter 5	170
Chapter 6	174

단계영어
백설공주

LEVEL 1

단어(Words)
611개 — Low / Middle / High

문장수(Sentences)
107개 — Low / Middle / High

문장길이(Sentence Length)
5.7 — Low / Middle / High

읽는 시간(Reading time)
2분 26초 — Low / Middle / High

말하는 시간(Speaking Time)
4분 42초 — Low / Middle / High

레벨 1 오디오북

Chapter 1

It was snowing outside.
A queen sat at a window.
She was sewing.

She wished to have a child as white as snow.

Soon she had a baby.
The baby was as white as snow.
But the queen died.

Chapter 2

One year later, the king remarried.

The new Queen was beautiful, but she had a bad heart.
She had a magic mirror.

She asked the mirror, "Magic mirror, who is the most beautiful woman?"

"It is you," the magic mirror answered.

But Snow White became more beautiful than the Queen.

One day, the Queen asked the magic mirror.
"Who is the most beautiful woman in the world?"

But this time, the mirror answered, "It is not you."

The Queen was very angry.
The Queen did not like Snow White.

The Queen called a hunter and ordered him,
"Kill Snow White!"

The hunter tried to kill Snow White.
But he could not kill Snow White.

Snow White ran away.
The hunter killed a bear instead of Snow White.

Chapter 3

Snow White ran away into the woods. Now she was alone.

When night came, Snow White felt terrible.
She cried and cried.
Finally, she fell asleep.

Morning came.
Snow White woke up.

She looked around
and found a path.
She began to walk along it.

Snow White found a small house.

She opened the door.
There were seven
spoons and forks on a table.

Chapter 4

Snow White was very hungry. She ate some food in the house.

She was so tired.
She lay down on a bed and soon fell asleep.

It was evening.
The owners of the house came back.
The owners were seven dwarfs.

The seven dwarfs found out that someone was there.

The first dwarf said, "Someone used my bed."

The seventh dwarf said,
"Someone is lying on my bed."
The seven dwarfs gathered
around the bed.

And they said,
"What a lovely young lady!"

The next morning,
the dwarfs listened to
Snow White's sad story.
They said,
"Stay here with us."

"Don't worry about the Queen.
We will take care of you!"

The next morning,
the dwarfs went to work.
They told her not to open the
door.

Chapter 5

The hunter returned to the Queen.
The hunter told the Queen that Snow White was dead.

The Queen was so happy.
But the magic mirror said, "Snow White is the most beautiful woman."
The Queen was very angry.

The Queen changed her clothes.
She looked like an old woman.
She went to the woods.
She found the little house.

The old woman knocked on the door.

"Who's there?" said Snow White.

"I'm selling apples."

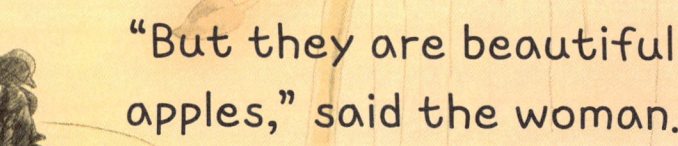

"I don't need any apples," Snow White said.

"But they are beautiful apples," said the woman.

"I cannot open the door to anyone," said Snow White.

"Good girl," the old woman said. "I will give you an apple as a gift."

Snow White opened the door.
She ate the apple.
She fell on the floor.

The Queen left.
But she fell into a swamp.
No one saw her.
She was gone.

Chapter 6

The weather was bad.
The dwarfs worried about Snow White.
The dwarfs ran to the house.

The dwarfs found Snow White.

The dwarfs cried and cried.
The dwarfs laid her on a bed of flowers.
They took her into the woods.
They went to see her every day.

One night, a young man came.
The young man was a Prince.
He said, "I will take her to my house. A doctor can help."

The Prince saw Snow White.
"She is pretty. I want to kiss her," he said.
The Prince kissed Snow White.
Snow White opened her eyes.

The Prince married Snow White.
The dwarfs said goodbye.
Snow White lived in a big house.

She was happy.

단계영어

백설공주

LEVEL 2

단어(Words)
819개 — Low

문장수(Sentences)
124개 — Low

문장길이(Sentence Length)
6.6 — Low

읽는 시간(Reading time)
3분 16초 — Low

말하는 시간(Speaking Time)
6분 18초 — Low

레벨 2 오디오북

Chapter 1

It was snowing outside.
A queen sat at a window.
She was sewing.
She pricked her finger with the needle.

Red blood fell on the cloth.
She wanted to have a child as white as snow.

Soon she had a little daughter.
The little daughter was as white as snow.
But when the little daughter was born, the queen died.

Chapter 2

One year later, the king got married again.
The new Queen was a beautiful woman, but her heart was not beautiful.
She had a great magic mirror.
She looked in the mirror and said,
"Who is the most beautiful woman in the world?"

The magic mirror answered,
"It is you, my Queen."
She was happy.

When Snow White was 17 years old, she became more beautiful than the Queen.

One day, the Queen asked the mirror, "Who is the most beautiful woman in the world?"
The magic mirror answered,
"It is not you, my Queen."

The Queen was very upset.
The Queen hated Snow White.

The Queen called a hunter.
She said to him,
"Kill Snow White!"

The hunter took out his knife and tried to kill Snow White.
She began to cry and said, "Please don't kill me."

The hunter didn't kill Snow White and said,
"Run away!"

But he thought, "The beasts will eat her." Then a little bear came to the hunter. He killed the bear instead of Snow White.

Chapter 3

Snow White ran away into the woods.
Now she was alone in the woods.

When night came, Snow White began to cry.
She felt terrible.
Finally, she fell asleep under a tree.

When morning came, the birds sang a song.
Snow White woke up too.

She looked around and found a path.
She walked along the path.

Snow White found a house.
It was a very small house.

She pushed the door open.
Everything in the house was small.
There were seven small spoons and small forks on a table.

Chapter 4

Snow White was so hungry and thirsty.
She ate some bread and drank juice.

She was so tired that she lay down on one of the beds.
She went to sleep.

When it was evening, the owners of the house came back.
They were the seven dwarfs who worked in the mountains.

The seven dwarfs found out that someone had touched their things.

Then the first dwarf looked around and said, "Someone used my bed."
The seventh dwarf looked at his bed and said,
"Someone is lying on my bed."

He called the other dwarfs and they gathered around the bed.
They cried out, "What a lovely young lady!"
They did not wake her up.

The next morning, the dwarfs heard Snow White's sad story. Then one of them said, "Stay here with us."

The dwarfs said, "You can live here. Don't worry about the Queen. We will take care of you!"

The next morning, the dwarfs went to work.
They told her not to open the door to anyone.

Chapter 5

At the same time, the hunter returned to the Queen.
He told the Queen that Snow White was dead.

The Queen was so happy.
She went to the magic mirror.
But the magic mirror said, "Snow White is the most beautiful woman."
The Queen was so angry that she went crazy.

The Queen changed herself to look like an old woman.
She went to the woods.
She found the house.

The old woman knocked on the door.
"Who's there?" said Snow White.
"I'm an old woman selling apples."
"I don't need any apples, thank you," Snow White said.

"But they are beautiful and juicy apples," said the woman.
"I cannot open the door to anyone," said Snow White.
"Good girl," the old woman said. "I will give you an apple as a gift."
Snow White opened the door just a little to take the apple.
She took a bite of the apple.
She fell to the ground.

The Queen left quickly.
But she fell into a swamp.
No one heard her.
She disappeared.

Chapter 6

Suddenly the weather turned bad.
The dwarfs worried about Snow White.
They ran fast to the house.

The dwarfs found Snow White.
She did not wake up.
They cried and cried.

They laid her on a bed of roses.
They took her into the woods.
They went to see her every day.

One night, a young man came to the woods.
The young man was a Prince.
He heard about Snow White.
He said,
"I will take her to my house.
A doctor can help her."

The Prince saw her.
He said, "She is so pretty. I want to kiss her."
He kissed Snow White.
Snow White opened her eyes.
She was alive!

The Prince loved Snow White.
He married Snow White.
The dwarfs said goodbye to Snow White.
Snow White lived in a big house.
She was happy.

단계영어

백설공주

LEVEL 3

단어(Words)
1275개 — Low / Middle / High

문장수(Sentences)
164개 — Low / Middle / High

문장길이(Sentence Length)
7.8 — Low / Middle / High

읽는 시간(Reading time)
5분 6초 — Low / Middle / High

말하는 시간(Speaking Time)
9분 48초 — Low / Middle / High

레벨 3 오디오북

Chapter 1

A long time ago, a queen sat at a window sewing. Outside the window, the snow was falling from the sky. The window was made of black wood. While she was sewing, she pricked her finger with the needle.

And red blood fell on the white cloth. The blood looked pretty on the cloth. She thought to herself, "I want to have a child as white as snow, with lips as red as blood."

Soon she had a little daughter who was as white as snow. Her lips were as red as blood. So she was called little Snow White. But when the child was born, the queen died.

Chapter 2

After a year had passed, the king took another wife for himself. She was a beautiful woman, but proud and arrogant. She had a fantastic magic mirror. It told the truth.

She stood in front of the magic mirror and said,
"Magic mirror on the wall, who is the most beautiful woman in the world?"
The magic mirror answered,
"My Queen, you are the most beautiful woman in the world."
Then she was happy.

But Snow White grew up. When she

was seventeen years old, she was more beautiful than the Queen.

One morning, the Queen asked the mirror,
"Magic mirror on the wall, who is the most beautiful woman in the world?"
The magic mirror answered,
"My Queen, Snow White is more beautiful than you."

Then
the Queen
was shocked and
turned red. When she
looked at Snow White, she sighed
deeply. The Queen hated Snow
White so much that she had no
peace.

She called a hunter and said, "Take
the child into the forest and kill

her."

The hunter took her away. He drew his knife and tried to kill her. She began to weep and said, "Let me have my life. I will never come home again."

The hunter felt sorry for her and said, "Run away, poor child."

But he thought, "There is no need to kill her. The wild beasts will eat her soon."

Just then, a little bear came running to the hunter. He killed it instead of Snow White.

Chapter 3

Now the poor child was all alone in the forest. She looked at the trees and did not know what to do. Then

she began to run again.

When night came, and Snow White began to cry loudly. She felt scary eyes spying on her, and she heard strange sounds. Finally, she fell asleep under a tree.

When morning came, the sound of birds filled the forest. Snow White woke up too. The forest was beautiful. Snow White was not afraid anymore.

However, the trees were like a wall around her. She tried to find a way

out. Snow White found a path.
She walked along it and came to a clearing.

There was a small house with a small door and small windows. Everything about the house was very small.

Snow White pushed the door open. Everything in the house was small. There was a white cloth on the table. Seven little plates, seven little spoons, seven little knives, and seven little forks were on the table. There were seven white beds.

Chapter 4

Snow White was so hungry and thirsty. She ate some bread from each plate and drank some juice from each cup.

Then, because she was so tired, she lay down on one of the little beds. But one bed was too long and another bed was too short. Finally, Snow White found the right one. She said a prayer and went to sleep.

When it was quite dark, the owners of the house came back.

They were seven dwarfs who were miners. They saw that someone had been there, because everything was moved around. The seven dwarfs said, "Someone has been eating our food and using our forks."

Then the first dwarf looked around and saw his bed. "Someone has been in my bed." The other dwarfs came over and each of them said, "Someone was lying in my bed too." But the seventh dwarf said, "Someone is sleeping in my bed."

He called the others, and they cried out with wonder. "Oh, my! What a lovely young lady!" They did not wake her up. They let her sleep. The seventh dwarf slept in another bed.

The next morning the dwarfs asked, "Who are you?"

Snow White told them her sad story. Then one of them said, "Stay here with us!"

"Yay! Hooray!" they cheered, dancing around the young lady. The dwarfs said to Snow White, "You can live here and take care of the house. Don't worry about the Queen. We love you! We will take care of you!"

Snow White accepted their kind offer. The next morning, the dwarfs

left for work. They told Snow White
not to open the door to strangers.

Meanwhile, the hunter returned to the castle. He told the Queen that Snow White was dead. He asked for the reward.

The Queen was very pleased. She spoke again to the magic mirror. But the magic mirror said, "The most beautiful woman in the land is Snow White." The Queen was so angry that she was overwhelmed. "She must die! She must die!" she cried out.

The Queen changed herself to look like a poor old woman. She put a poisoned apple in her basket. She went quickly into the forest. She crossed the swamp. She arrived at the house. Just as Snow White waved goodbye to the seven dwarfs.

Snow White heard a sound at the door, KNOCK! KNOCK!

"Who's there?" she said.

"I'm a poor old woman selling apples," the voice said.

"I don't need any apples, thank you," Snow White said.

"But they are beautiful, juicy apples!" said the voice from outside the door.

"I can't open the door for anyone," said Snow White.

"That's right! You can't open

the door for strangers, so you can't buy anything. You are a good girl!"

Then the old woman said,
"As a reward for being good, I will give you an apple as a gift!"

Snow White opened the door just a tiny bit to take the apple.

"Look! That's a good apple."
Snow White bit into the fruit. She fell to the ground.

The evil Queen left in a hurry. But when she crossed the swamp, she tripped and fell in. No one heard her. No one helped her. She disappeared.

Chapter 6

Meanwhile, the sky was dark. There was a flash of lightning in the sky. There was loud thunder. The dwarfs worried about Snow White. They ran to the house quickly.

They found Snow White lying on the floor of the house. They found the poisoned apple. They cried and cried for a long time. They laid her on a bed of roses. They carried her into the forest. They put a flower there every day.

One evening, a young man came

to the forest. The young man was a Prince. He saw Snow White lying there. He heard her story. He said, "I will take her to my castle to get help from a doctor."

The Prince saw her again. He said, "She's beautiful... I wish I could kiss her!" He did. The kiss broke the spell. Snow White opened her eyes. She was alive again!

The Prince asked Snow White to marry him. The dwarfs said goodbye to Snow White. Snow White was so happy to live in a big castle. She liked to visit her friends in the forest.

단계영어

백설공주

LEVEL 4

단어(Words)
1732개
Low　　　　Middle　　　　High

문장수(Sentences)
194개
Low　　　　Middle　　　　High

문장길이(Sentence Length)
8.9
Low　　　　Middle　　　　High

읽는 시간(Reading time)
6분 55초
Low　　　　Middle　　　　High

말하는 시간(Speaking Time)
13분 19초
Low　　　　Middle　　　　High

레벨 4 오디오북

Chapter 1

Once upon a time, a queen sat at a window sewing. Outside the window, the snow was falling like feathers from the sky. The frame of the window was made of black wood. While she was sewing and looking out of the window, she

pricked her finger with the needle.

And three drops of blood fell on the white cloth. The red blood looked pretty on the white cloth. She thought to herself, "I want to have a child as white as snow, with lips as red as blood, and hair as black as the wood of the window-frame."

Soon after that, she had a little daughter who was as white as snow. Her lips were as red as blood, and her hair was as black as the wood of the window frame. She was called little Snow White. However, when the child was born, the queen died.

Chapter 2

After a year had passed, the king took another wife for himself. She was a beautiful woman, but proud and arrogant. She could not bear anyone who was more beautiful than she was. She had a fantastic magic mirror. It told the truth.

When she stood in front of it, she said,

"Magic mirror, magic mirror on the wall, who is the fairest woman in the world?"

The magic mirror answered,

"My Queen, you are the fairest woman in the world."

Then she was satisfied, because the mirror only told the truth.

But Snow White grew up and became more and more beautiful. When Snow White was seventeen years old, she was more beautiful than the Queen.

One morning, the Queen asked the mirror,
"Magic mirror on the wall, who is the fairest woman in the world?"
It answered,
"Oh, Lady Queen, Snow White is fairer than

you."

Then the Queen was shocked and she turned yellow and green. Whenever she looked at Snow White, she sighed deeply. The Queen hated the girl so much. Her envy and pride grew higher and higher. She had no peace day or night.

She called a hunter and said, "Take the child away into the forest. I don't want to see her anymore. Kill her, and bring me back her heart."

The hunter obeyed and took her away. But as he drew his knife and tried to kill Snow White, she began to weep, and said,

"Ah, dear hunter, let me have my life. I will run away into the forest, and never come home again."

The hunter felt sorry for her and said, "Run away, poor child."

But he thought, "The wild beasts will eat her soon." He felt peace since he did not need to kill her. Just then, a little bear came running up to him, and he killed it with a knife. He cut out its heart and took it to the Queen.

Chapter 3

Now the poor child was all alone in the dark forest. She looked at all the leaves on the trees and she did not know what to do. Then she began to run again and she ran until it was almost evening.

Night came, and Snow White began to cry loudly. She felt terrible eyes spying on her, and she heard strange sounds that made her heart pound. At last, overcome by tiredness, she fell asleep under a tree.

Finally, dawn broke and the song of the birds filled the forest. Snow White woke up too. The dark forest was full of life. And now she realized she did not need to be afraid.

However, the thick trees were like a wall around her. And as she tried to find a way out, she came upon a path. She walked along it. She walked until she came to a clearing.

There was a strange cottage with a tiny door and tiny windows. Everything about the cottage was much smaller than normal.

Snow White pushed the door open. Everything in the cottage was small, but cleaner than can be told. There was a white cloth on the table. Seven little plates, seven little spoons, seven little knives, seven little forks, and seven little cups were on the table. There were seven little beds side by side. They were covered with blankets that were white like snow.

Chapter 4

Snow White was so hungry and thirsty. She ate some vegetables and bread from each plate and drank juice from each cup. She did not want to eat and drink everything from one plate or cup.

Then, because she was so tired, she laid herself down on one of the little beds. None of them were the right size for her. One bed was too long and another bed was too short. At last, Snow White found that the seventh bed was just right. She rested on that bed. She said a prayer and went to sleep.

When it was quite dark, the owners of the cottage came back. They were seven dwarfs who dug deep in the mountains for metal. They had seven candles. They saw that someone had been there, because everything was not in the same place where they left it.

The first dwarf said,

"Who has been sitting on my chair?"

The second dwarf said,

"Who has been eating off my plate?"

The third dwarf said,

"Who has been eating some of my bread?"

The fourth dwarf said,

"Who has been eating my vegetables?"

The fifth dwarf said,

"Who has been using my fork?"

The sixth dwarf said,

"Who has been cutting with my knife?"

The seventh dwarf said,

"Who has been drinking out of my cup?"

Then the first dwarf looked around and saw that there was something different about his bed.

"Someone was sleeping in my bed."

The other dwarfs came over and each of them said,

"Someone was lying in my bed too."

But when the seventh dwarf looked at his bed, he saw Snow White sleeping on it. He called the others, and they cried out with surprise. They brought their seven little candles with them.

"Oh my goodness! What a lovely young lady!"

They were so glad they did not wake

her up. They let her sleep in the bed. The seventh dwarf shared a bed with one of the others.

The next morning the dwarfs asked the little girl,
"Who are you?"
Snow White told them her sad story. They cried many tears. Then one of the dwarfs blew his nose.
"Stay here with us!" he said.

"Hooray! Hooray!" they cheered, dancing joyfully around the little girl.

The dwarfs said to Snow White, "You can live here and take care of the house while we work. Don't worry about the Queen. We love you and we will take care of you!"

Snow White was grateful. She accepted their kind offer. The next morning, the dwarfs left for work. They told Snow White not to open the door to strangers.

Chapter 5

Meanwhile, the hunter had returned to the castle. He gave the heart of the little bear to the Queen. He told her it was Snow White's. He wanted to claim the reward.

The Queen was very pleased. She turned again to the magic mirror.

But the mirror said, "The loveliest woman in the land is still Snow White, who lives with the seven dwarfs."

The Queen was extremely angry. She lost her mind. "She must die! She must die!" she screamed.

The Queen disguised herself as an old peasant woman. She put a poisoned apple in her basket. Then, she went quickly into the forest and crossed the swamp. Just as she arrived, Snow White waved good-bye to the seven dwarfs.

Snow White was in the kitchen when she heard the sound at the door, KNOCK! KNOCK!

"Who's there?" she said. She remembered the dwarfs' advice.

"I'm an old peasant woman selling apples," the voice replied.

"I don't need any apples, thank you," Snow White replied.

"But they are beautiful apples and they are so juicy!" said the smooth voice from outside the door.

"I should not open the door for anyone," said Snow White. She did not want to ignore what the dwarfs said.

"You are right! Good girl! You can't buy anything if you promised not to open the door for strangers. You are a good girl!"

Then the old woman continued.

"As a reward for being good, I'm going to give you an apple as a gift!"
Right away, Snow White opened the door just a tiny bit to take the apple.

"There! That's a nice apple, isn't it?"
Snow White bit into the fruit. She fainted and fell to the ground. The poison killed her quickly.

The evil Queen hurried away. She ran back across the swamp. She tripped and fell into some quicksand. No one heard her call for help. She disappeared. No one could find her.

Chapter 6

Meanwhile, the dwarfs came out of the mine. They saw that the sky was dark and stormy. Thunder made loud sounds in the valleys and lightning ripped through the sky. They were worried about Snow White. They quickly ran to the cottage.

At the cottage, they found Snow White. She was lying there, lifeless. The poisoned apple was by her side. They tried their best to wake her up, but nothing worked. They wept and wept for a long time. Then they laid her on a bed of rose petals. They carried her into the forest and put her in a glass coffin. They placed a flower there each day.

One evening, a young man came upon them. He looked at Snow White's pretty face through the glass. The man was a Prince! He heard Snow White's story, and he had an idea. "If you allow me to take her to my castle, I will bring in doctors. They will wake her up from this strange sleep."

The Prince saw her again, and he said, "She's so lovely... I wish I could kiss her!" He did. It was magic. The Prince's kiss broke the spell. Everyone was surprised. Snow White opened her eyes. She came back to life!

The Prince was in love. He asked Snow White to marry him. The dwarfs were sad to see her go. They said goodbye to Snow White. Snow White lived in the great castle. She was very happy. But she remembered the little cottage. Sometimes she went to the forest to visit her friends.

단계영어

백설공주

LEVEL 5

단어(Words)

문장수(Sentences)

문장길이(Sentence Length)

읽는 시간(Reading time)

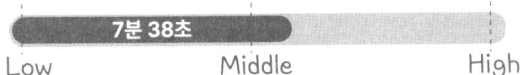

말하는 시간(Speaking Time)

THE ORIGINAL TEXT

레벨 5 오디오북

Chapter 1

Once upon a time, a queen sat at a window sewing. Outside the window, the flakes of snow were falling like feathers from the sky. The frame of the window was made of black ebony. While she was sewing and looking out of the window, she pricked her finger with the needle.

And three drops of blood fell upon the white cloth. The red looked pretty upon the white cloth, and she thought to herself, "I wish that I could have a child as white as snow, with lips as red as blood, and hair as black as the ebony frame."

Soon after that, she had a little daughter who was as white as snow. Her lips were as red as blood, and her hair was as black as ebony, and she was called little Snow White. However, when the child was born, the queen died.

Chapter 2

After a year had passed, the king took another wife for himself. She was a beautiful woman, but proud and arrogant, and she could not bear anyone else who was more beautiful than she was. She had a magnificent magic mirror. It could answer questions truthfully.

When she stood in front of it and looked at herself in it, and said,
"Magic mirror, magic mirror on the wall, who is the fairest in the world?"

The magic mirror answered,
"My Queen, you are the fairest woman in the world."
Then she was satisfied, for she knew that the magic mirror spoke the truth.

But Snow White grew up and became more and more beautiful. When Snow White was seventeen years old, she was more beautiful than the Queen.

One morning, the Queen asked the mirror,
"Magic mirror on the wall, who is the fairest woman in the world?"
It answered,
"Oh, Lady Queen, Snow White is fairer than you."

Then the Queen was shocked and turned yellow and green with envy. From that moment, whenever she looked at Snow White, her heart pounded in her chest. The Queen hated the girl so much. And envy and pride grew higher and higher in her heart like a weed. She had no peace day or night.

She called a hunter and said, "Take the child

away into the forest. I will no longer have her here. Kill her, and bring me back her heart as a present."

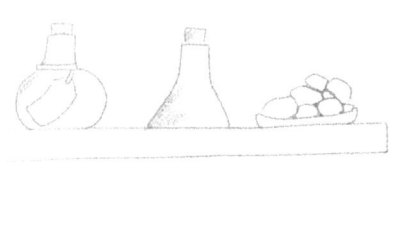

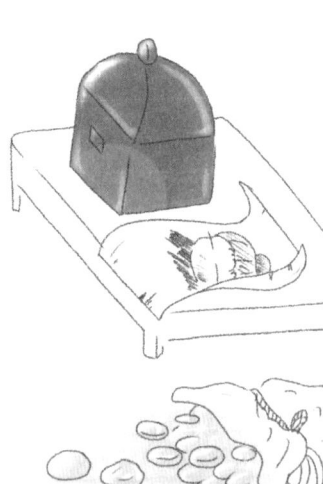

The hunter obeyed and

took her away, but as he drew his knife and tried to pierce Snow White's innocent heart, she began to weep, and said,

"Ah, dear hunter, let me have my life. I will run away into the wild forest, and never come home again."

Because she was so beautiful, the hunter felt sorry for her and said,

"Run away, poor child."

But he thought, "The wild beasts will eat her soon."

Yet he felt at peace, since he did not need to kill her. Just then, a little bear came running up to him, and he stabbed it. He cut out its heart and took it to the Queen to show that Snow White was dead.

Chapter 3

Now the poor child was all alone in the dark forest. She looked at all the leaves on the trees and she did not know what to do. Then she began to run and she ran for as long as she could, until it was almost evening.

Night came, and Snow White began to cry

loudly. She thought she felt terrible eyes spying on her, and she heard strange sounds that made her heart thump. At last, overcome by tiredness, she fell asleep curled under a tree.

Finally, dawn came and the song of the birds came to the forest. Snow White also woke up. The whole world was coming to life. She was happy to realize that she did not need to be afraid.

However, the thick trees were like a wall around her. And as she tried to find out where she was, she came upon a path. She walked along and felt hope. She walked until she came to a clearing.

There stood a strange cottage, with a tiny

door, tiny windows, and a tiny chimney. Everything about the cottage was much smaller than a normal house.

Snow White pushed the door open. Everything in the cottage was small, but the cottage was neat and clean. There was a white cloth on the table. Seven little plates, seven little spoons, seven little knives, seven little forks, and seven little cups were on the table. There were seven little beds side by side against the wall. They were covered with blankets that were white like snow.

Chapter 4

Snow White was so hungry and thirsty that she ate some vegetables and bread from each plate and drank a drop of juice out of each cup. She did not want to eat and drink everything from one plate or cup.

Then, because she was so tired, she laid herself down on one of the little beds. None of them were the right size for her. One bed was too long and another bed was too short. At last, Snow White found out that the seventh one was just right. She rested on that bed. She said a prayer and went to sleep.

When it was quite dark, the owners of the cottage came back. They were seven dwarfs who dug deep in the mountains for ore. They lit seven candles. The light was bright inside the cottage. They saw that someone had been there, because everything was not as they had left it.

The first dwarf said,
"Who has been sitting on my chair?"
The second dwarf said,
"Who has been eating off my plate?"
The third dwarf said,
"Who has been eating some of my bread?"

The fourth dwarf said,
"Who has been eating my vegetables?"
The fifth dwarf said,
"Who has been using my fork?"
The sixth dwarf said,
"Who has been cutting with my knife?"
The seventh dwarf said,
"Who has been drinking out of my cup?"

 Then the first dwarf looked around and saw that something was different about his bed.
"Someone was sleeping in my bed."
The other dwarfs came over and each of them said, "Someone was lying in my bed too."
But when the seventh dwarf looked at his bed,

he saw little Snow White sleeping there.

He called the others, who came running up, and they cried out with shock. They brought their seven little candles and let the light shine on little Snow White.
"Oh heavens! Oh heavens! What a lovely young lady!"
They were so glad they did not wake her up, and they let her keep sleeping in the bed. The seventh dwarf couldn't find a place to sleep, so he took turns sleeping in his friends' beds, spending one hour in each.

The next morning the dwarfs asked the little girl, "Who are you?"
Snow White told them her sad story. Tears came to their eyes. Then one of the dwarfs said, "Stay here with us!" as he blew his nose.

"Hooray! Hooray!" they cheered, dancing joyfully around the little girl. The dwarfs said to Snow White, "You can live here and take care of the house while we work in the mine. Don't worry about the Queen. We love you and we will take care of you!"

Snow White was grateful. She accepted their hospitality, and the next morning the dwarfs went off to work. They told Snow White not to open the door to strangers.

Chapter 5

Meanwhile, the hunter had returned to the castle with the heart of the little bear. He gave it to the cruel Queen. He told her it was Snow White's so that he could claim the reward.

The Queen turned to the magic mirror, very pleased. But her hopes were crushed. The mirror said to her, "The loveliest woman in the land is still Snow White, who lives with the seven dwarfs in the forest."
The Queen was beside herself with anger.
"She must die! She must die!" she screamed.

The Queen disguised herself as an old peasant woman. She put a poisoned apple with other apples into a basket. Then, she took the quickest way into the forest. She crossed the swamp at the edge of the trees. She reached the far side, unseen. At this moment, Snow White was waving goodbye to the dwarfs on their way to the mine.

Snow White was in the kitchen when she heard a sound at the door, KNOCK! KNOCK!

"Who's there?" she said. She remembered the dwarfs' advice.

"I'm an old peasant woman selling apples," the voice replied.

"I don't need any apples, thank you," Snow White replied.

"But they are beautiful apples and they are so juicy!" said the smooth voice from outside the door.

"I shouldn't open the door for anyone," said Snow White. She did not want to disobey her friends.

"You're right! You're such a good girl! If you promised not to open the door for strangers, then you can't buy anything. Yes, you're a good girl!"

Then the old woman continued. "As a reward for being good, I'm going to give you one of my apples as a gift!"

Snow White did not think about it. She opened the door just a tiny crack to take the apple.

"There! Isn't that a nice apple?" Snow White bit into the fruit, and as she did, she fell to the ground. The terrible poison killed her right away.

The evil Queen laughed and hurried away. But when she ran back across the swamp, she tripped and fell into some quicksand. No one heard her cries for help. She disappeared and no one could find her.

Chapter 6

Meanwhile, the dwarfs came out of the mine. They saw that the sky was dark and stormy. Thunder echoed through the valleys, and streaks of lightning ripped through the sky. They were worried about Snow White and they ran down the mountain as quickly as they could. They arrived at the cottage.

At the cottage, they found Snow White. She was lying there dead with the poisoned apple by her side. They tried their best to bring her to life, but it was no use. They wept and wept for a long time.

Then they laid her on a bed of petals. They carried her into the forest and put her in a glass coffin. They placed a flower there each day.

One evening, they came upon a young man looking at Snow White's beautiful face through the glass. This man was a Prince! After he heard her story, he made a suggestion.
"If you allow me to take her to my castle, I will bring in famous doctors. They will wake her up from this unusual sleep."

The Prince saw her again, and he said, "She's so lovely... I wish I could kiss her!" He did. Something magical happened! The Prince's kiss broke the spell! Everyone was amazed. Snow White opened her eyes. She came back to life!

The Prince was in love. He asked Snow White to marry him. The dwarfs were sad to say goodbye to Snow White. Snow White lived a happy life in the great castle. But she always remembered the little cottage in the forest. She went back to visit her friends there whenever she could.